My New Dog

WAYLAND

First published in 2011
by Wayland

Text copyright © Claire Llewellyn
Photograph copyright © Wayland
with the exception of background
pawprints (throughout) and folio
graphic (throughout) both © Istock

Wayland
338 Euston Road
London NW1 3BH

Wayland Australia
Level 17/207 Kent Street
Sydney, NSW 2000

Series Editor: Louise John
Editor: Katie Powell
Design: D.R.ink
Photographer: Andy Crawford
Consultant: Shirley Bickler

A CIP catalogue record for this book is
available from the British Library.

ISBN 9780750263771

Printed in China

Wayland is a division of Hachette Children's Books,
an Hachette UK Company

www.hachette.co.uk

With thanks to the Oxfordshire Animal
Sanctury Society, Pets at Home and Dotty the dog

Every effort has been made to clear copyright.
Should there be any inadvertent omission,
please apply to the publisher for rectification.

Contents

Meet Jess

I have a new pet!
She is a dog called Jess.

Jess was at a rescue centre
and she needed a new home.

The rescue centre

Mum, Dad, my sister and I went
to the rescue centre.

OXFORDSHIRE
ANIMAL SANCTUARY
SOCIETY

A lady called Emma showed us
all the dogs. We liked Jess the best!

A good pet

We told Emma that we wanted to give Jess a home.

"Jess likes children," said Emma.
"She will be a good pet."

The house visit

The next day Emma came to our house.

She looked at the garden.

She said, "This will be a good home for Jess. She will be safe here."

At the pet shop

We all went to the pet shop
to get things for Jess.

Lead

Dog bowl

We got a lead, a dog
bowl, a ball and lots
of other things.

Getting Jess

Then we went to get Jess.
Emma got her out of her kennel.
"Goodbye, Jess," she said.

Mum put Jess in the car
and we drove away.
Jess was our dog now!

Jess comes home

It was fun bringing Jess home.
First she had a drink.

Then she had a run in the garden.
"She likes the garden," said Mum.

Walking Jess

Jess needs a walk every day.
Today we took her to the park.

Mum let me hold the lead.

A good friend

I like looking after Jess. I brush her coat and I play with her.

Dog brush

Dog bed

Jess likes me, too.
We are good friends.

Tell the story

These photos will help you tell the story of my new dog. Can you put them in the right order?

START READING is a series of highly enjoyable books for beginner readers. **The books have been carefully graded to match the Book Bands widely used in schools.** This enables readers to be sure they choose books that match their own reading ability.

Look out for the Band colour on the book in our Start Reading logo.

The Bands are:

Pink Band 1A & 1B

Red Band 2

Yellow Band 3

Blue Band 4

Green Band 5

Orange Band 6

Turquoise Band 7

Purple Band 8

Gold Band 9

START READING books can be read independently or shared with an adult. They promote the enjoyment of reading through satisfying stories and non-fiction narratives, which are supported by fun illustrations and photographs.

Claire Llewellyn has written many books for children. Some of them are about real things like animals and the Moon, others are storybooks. Claire has two children, but they are getting too big for her books now. She hopes you will enjoy reading them instead!